TERRY WOGAN'S
BUMPER BOOK OF TOGS

TERRY WOGAN'S

Published by BBC Books,
a division of BBC Worldwide Limited,
Woodlands, 80 Wood Lane,
London W12 OTT.

First published 1995
Reprinted 1995

ISBN 0 563 38735 1

Set in News Gothic and Century Old Style by Ace Filmsetting Ltd, Frome

Printed and bound in Great Britain by Butler & Tanner Ltd, Frome and London

Jacket printed by Lawrence Allen Ltd, Weston-super-Mare

BUMPER BOOK OF TOGS

CONTENTS

PREFACE

Having spent endless years on television presenting varicose 'award' shows, I grew to view with a rheumy eye the actor or actress who would shyly step up to receive their accolade and, despite having known for at least a fortnight that they had won, would laughingly blurt: 'Oh gosh! Help! I don't know what to say . . . Thank you, thank you . . .' and nip off with the prize, leaving the producer also speechless, but with rage, and a minute and a half of his programme to fill . . .

But as the old Radio 2 crowd-pleaser has it: 'Where do I begin?' With my parents, Michael and Rose? With the light of my life, Helen? With the wonderful Jo Gurnett? Maybe with Charmaine Dobson, whose enthusiasm pushed the whole thing through at breakneck speed. And then there are Heather and Frank and all of BBC Worldwide Publishing, without whom – zippo . . . Where do you leave Gray Jolliffe, with his huge-nosed, bug-eyed, wobbly characters? The man can't draw a straight line . . . but he's got those geezers and gals off to a T – for TOG, of course.

The TOGs? This book wouldn't be disgracing these shelves without them. Radio 2 between 7.30 and 9.30 every week-day morning would be quiet as the grave, its presenter sitting there in front of the microphone, mumchance . . . The TOGs are my inspiration, my constant joy, my reason to get up in the morning. We could fill a hundred books a year with their effusions, their inspired outpourings of fantasy and fun. Bless 'em all . . .

It's my devout wish that this simple, homespun volume, culled from some of the most demented and bewildered writings of the present century, will provide you, gentle reader, with many hours of innocent enjoyment . . .

Proving once again, if indeed proof were needed, that most uplifting of all the TOG adages:

They're Not All Locked Up Yet . . .

Va, Pensiero!
(Go, Old One!)

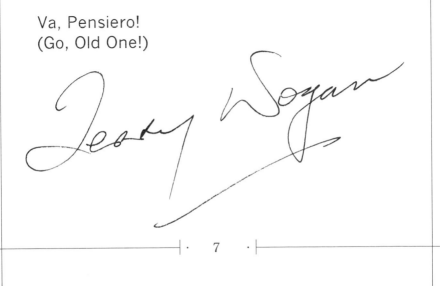

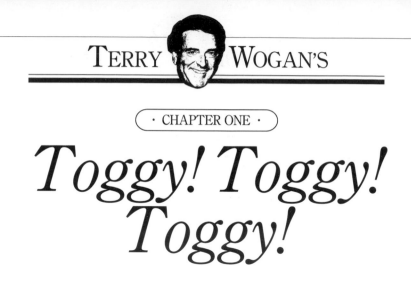

· CHAPTER ONE ·

Toggy! Toggy! Toggy!

WHAT IS A TOG?

FOR ONCE, CHAMBERS, Webster's and the Oxford dictionaries are of one mind.

TOGs: Terry's Old Geezers/Terry's Old Gals. Listeners to *Wake Up To Wogan* 7.30–9.30 a.m., Monday to Friday, BBC Radio 2. Thought to be the direct descendants of the TWITS (Terry Wogan is Tops Society), a movement which flourished in the mid-1970s.

TOGs are well stricken in years and fiercely proud of it. They deeply resent the efforts of younger people (TYGs – Terry's Young Geezers) to infiltrate the coven. The piteous pleadings of such youngsters are invariably spurned with a brusque 'Clear off, you young limb!'

TOGS come in many guises, but are most readily recognized by their chant 'Toggy! Toggy! Toggy!' and the secret TOG sign, known only to those who see it flashed on the radio by Wogan every morning. There is an even more secret Grand Master TOG sign, always exchanged under cover of darkness and known only to Wogan himself, ailing producer, Poorly Walters, and the Duke of Kent.

I came downstairs to help me remember what I went upstairs for..

TOGS may also be recognized by their use of such arcane phrases as 'Is it me?', 'They don't know they're born', 'I never saw a bar of chocolate until I was fourteen' and 'Why did I come upstairs?'

LET THE TOGS IDENTIFY THEMSELVES!

A TOGs car-sticker is another method of identification, but is rarely seen other than on Reliant Robins, Morris Mini-Travellers, or zimmer frames. A competition to find a motif for the TOGs car-sticker produced the winning slogan:

> ## 'I STOP FOR NO PARTICULAR REASON . . .'

But here! Why waste time with dry-as-dust dictionary definitions? Let the TOGs speak for themselves!

It takes me four goes to put on my vest,
It's been six weeks since I last had a snog,
I'm the only one who remembers George Best,
Oh, no! I'm becoming a TOG.

John Machin, Cheshire

• • •

TOGs

We decided to start our own local branch of TOGs, and the very first meeting took place last week.

The session started with a game, to break the ice, of 'I Spy'. This proved to be a mistake because most of the members had forgotten to bring their glasses.

Undeterred, we decided to be more daring – the men then threw their false teeth into the middle of the carpet and the ladies had to pick a denture and pair off with its owner. They then adjourned to other rooms to discuss their operations.

We ended with a raffle, first prize of which was a knitted pension book cover.

Pauline Lynch, Norfolk

WHEREAS SOME, LIKE John Walker of Birmingham, display symptoms of mild panic.

Dear Tog-Chieftain,

I nsidious symptoms have begun to present themselves.

Lissom beauties no longer seem to regard me as a threat. I have recently taken up growing fuchsias, tapestry work and my back hurts. I wear a duster coat when I do woodwork and I can't open those widget-type cans without spraying everyone in sight with beer. I have also become disenchanted with soccer and have taken to watching rugby, even though I can't understand it.

Does all this mean I am becoming a TOG?

· · ·

HERMAN HUNCHTROUSER OF Erlow
cuts through the doubts and
fears.

. . .

A TOG is . . . always having to say you're sorry.

A TOG is . . . a wealth of knowledge, all of it useless.

A TOG . . . always tells the truth if he can remember it.

A TOG . . . always stands up for others, always
assuming he has a zimmer.

TOGs are . . . like a cream cracker: square, crumbly at
the edges and not much good on their own!

*The crystal-clear mind.
of the truly barking...*

THE LOYAL TOG is ever conscious of his status and will fight the imposter and interloper to his dying wheeze.

. . .

W hat's going on? Who issues the TOG car-stickers for you? What checks are made on the people who ask for them? How do you know they are real TOGs?

I ask because yesterday I saw a TOG car-sticker in the window of a snazzy sports car driven by a man, no older than twenty-five, wearing a baggy double-breasted suit and sporting an earring. I challenged him with the TOG sign and got no response. On further questioning and the threat of a cuff round the ear, he confessed to being an imposter, nay, a counterfeit TOG!

I suggest the following practical and written tests for all who aspire to TOGdom and a TOG car-sticker.

PRACTICAL

1. Give the TOG sign in at least two languages.

2. Light a coal fire without using firelighters or wood.

3. Find Radio Caroline on the wireless.

4. Be unable to touch your toes (or even see them), operate a video, use a PC or understand the Internet.

Touch my knees? What, with my legs straight?

WRITTEN

1. Who makes Desperate Dan's cow pies?
A: His Aunt Aggie (this is a test of long-term memory).

2. How much is one hundredweight and six pounds of coal at one florin and one farthing a pound?
A: £11 18s. 5½ d.

3. Who is the leader of the Labour Party?
A: Any answer except Tony Blair will suffice, showing typical TOG lack of short-term memory. Acceptable answers are Clem Attlee, Nye Bevan and Keir Hardie.

Hope this helps keep the TOG population unsullied by posturing youth, Tel.

Des Gusted, Kent

TOGS ARE PROUD folk, with a keen sense of history and a ready appreciation of those who have gone before.

I have started to compile a volume of *Great TOGs of Our Times*. It will, of course, include such greats as:

☆ GEORGE STEPHENSON who wanted to invent the railway but got so confused with the instructions that he invented the anorak instead.

☆ ETHELRED THE UNREADY who was, in fact, ready all the time but whose wife said he couldn't possibly go out in those shoes with those trousers and that shirt and sent him upstairs to get changed.

☆ ROBERT THE BRUCE who thought the persistent spider was a trailer for the next David Attenborough wildlife programme on BBC 1, having completely forgotten that television hadn't yet been invented.

Willy Eckerslike, West Yorkshire

. . .

It seems to me it is high time you thought of remembering some of the great TOGs of the past, without whom we would not find ourselves in the mess we are in today. In order to get the ball rolling, I have listed a few of the more notable among them, with brief notes on some of their major achievements.

ATTILA THE TOG

Who liked to rape and pillage, but who would stop without warning.

DAVID TOGGLESTONE

Famous explorer who found a great waterfall while wandering through the African bush one day and named it after the sponge cake he was eating at the time.

DAVID TOG-GEORGE

Prime Minister who introduced the Old Tog Pension in 1908.

ADMIRAL HORATIO TOGSON

Who died in Trafalgar Square when a pigeon flew into his good eye, causing him to fall off his column.

FIELD MARSHAL TOGGOMERY OF ALAMEIN

Who helped organize the Normandy landing where the famous Togberry floating harbours were used to get the King's Own Regiment of Togaliers ashore without getting their zimmer frames wet.

SIR OLIVER TOGWELL

Who was famous for his round head and chasing King Charles up oak trees and into four-poster beds.

SIR FRANCIS TOG

Elizabethan Toganeer who was playing bowls one day in Plymouth and spotted an armada of Spanish TOGs on their way to a Saga holiday in Bridlington and told them to tog off.

NURSE FLORENCE TOGGINGALE

Who used her lamp in Crimea, to pick out TOG casualties and tune their hospital radios into Radio 2 while they weren't looking.

AL CATOG

Who flooded Chicago with bootleg Sanatogen during prohibition years.

WILLIAM TOGSPEARE

Famous playwright who produced such masterpieces as *The Taming of the Tog*, *A Midsummer Night's Tog*, and *Romeo and Toglet*.

TOGGLONI

Famous inventor who succeeded in transmitting a radio message across the Atlantic in 1901, which was received by a young Terry Wogan who was sitting on a hill in Cornwall playing with his cat's whiskers.

Hugh Hunt, Hants

WITH LOSS OF short-term memory, days long-gone seem to appear in sharp relief. Ann O. Domini of Twilight House, London, struck a responsive and tearful chord in many a TOG's heart with these gentle memories of times past.

I am ninety-four, and when we were children my three sisters and I were given a farthing's worth of chips to share as a treat every Friday night. After we'd eaten the chips we'd have to give the newspaper they were wrapped in to my father. While he was reading it, my mother, sisters and I would fetch the zinc bath into the scullery for our weekly wash.

When my father had finished reading the newspaper he'd go down to the pub, and my sisters and I would spread the paper on the floor and take the coal out of the bath, lump by lump, placing it neatly on the paper. If the coalman had just been, this could take quite a long time. Meanwhile my mother would heat a bucket of rainwater on the stove. Then she would pour it into the bath, and we'd all get in it together to raise the water level and make the water go further.

When we got out, the bath water would be black with coal dust and my mother would pour it back in the bucket and keep it for blacking the scuffed patches on our shoes, and for disguising her grey

Continued next page

hairs. Then she would dry us with scraps of brown paper grocery bags she'd begged from the corner shop – we couldn't afford towels. We couldn't afford more than one bath load of coal a year either, so she'd dry out these pieces of paper and use them for fire-bricks when the coal ran out. Sometimes she'd use them for curling papers first – she was quite a vain woman.

After our bath we children would put the coal back in the bath and carry it outside again. How we used to look forward to Friday night! It was the highlight of our week. You'd never hear us complaining we'd no television.

. . .

ah, me . . .

TERRY WOGAN'S

DON'T BE DECEIVED by that TOG, crouched behind the wheel of his Volvo in flat cap and pipe. He may not be moving very fast in the middle lane, but, beneath the calm, even slightly dazed exterior, a maelstrom of vital juices are bubbling with pent-up energy – ideas for television.

. . .

How about an Old Geezers' TV game show, hosted by yourself or a younger person, like Lord Hailsham? The games could include such mind-numbing fun as . . .

THE OPEN FRIDGE DOOR: contestants have to try and remember if they are putting something in the fridge or taking something out.

THE MYSTERY OF THE SHOELACES: contestants have to tie a pair of shoelaces without having one bit of lace three-feet long and the other bit half-an-inch.

REMOTE CONTROL: contestants have to successfully increase volume and change station by using a remote control. This would be the longest game on the show and would incur the star prize of a mug tree.

THE SOCK CHALLENGE: a difficult one . . . From a drawer full of socks contestants have to match at least one pair of socks. Something that, in real life, is a very difficult thing to do.

Darryl Lane, Staffs

. . .

TOGIATORS READY!

T wo elderly members of your following, one male and one female, are 'togged' out in Lycra all-in-one suits with running shoes, harnesses, go-faster stripes and those other trimmings of the athletic types.

Meanwhile you, Terry, and that nice lady that fills in for you nine months of the year while you are on holiday, arc also sportily clad but with a certain lack of that 'competitive look'.

You introduce the programme to viewers and the hordes of screaming spectators around the arena, that no longer need to pay for bus fares, to the lucky competitors and also to their rivals . . .

To screams, cheers and a shower of lace hankies and walking sticks you introduce, one by one, the togiators!

PHILOSAN, GALLOWAYS, WRINKLE,
THERMAL, ZIMMER AND CORSET.

The crowd and viewers then proceed to enjoy the spectacle of octogenarians knocking each other off twenty-feet high pedestals, chasing each other up artificial cliff faces, assault course races and certain types of pseudo-rugby games.

The running time would be something like three hours! And I would advise having oxygen and the Red Cross present, and trying not to let Age Concern get hold of the publicity leaflets.

Peter Duhig, Norfolk

THEN, LO AND behold, up comes Stuart Nunn of Bristol with an idea to shake every Home For The Bewildered to its very foundations.

A TOGs Theme Park

Noel Edmonds has his Crinkley Bottom, our park should be called 'Wrinkly Valley'.

Special facilities at Wrinkly Valley would include rocking chairs instead of park benches, moving walkways from place to place and special patrols, not of police but of nurses, in case anyone gets a little over-excited.

Events might include three-legged zimmer race (tie the zimmers together instead of the legs); the cod-liver oil and spoon race; and the gunge tank equivalent – the Old Geezer phlegm tank.

Amusements would include the special big wheel where you clip on your wheelchair, and you're off. Then you could walk around a miniature village, comprising trees, grass, houses and a church, all made completely of wool by a group of knitting Old Geezers.

The ultimate highlight of the day, of course, would be the Shaky Arrows – a crack wheelchair display team.

. . .

a whole new can of worms was opened up.....

A Visit to Wrinkly Valley

We shall cruise down to the station in the Volvo and take the train to Wrinkly Valley. A real steam train with Pullman seats and a proper dining car. There'll be a Ladies' Waiting Room on the platform, a porter to carry our bags, and a car park with spaces in.

We will take a tram or perhaps a trolley-bus from the station. It will cost 1½d. In the street there will be cars with running-boards and semaphore indicators, and motorbikes with sidecars.

In the morning, a shopping trip on the main street. Lovely department stores, with counters where you don't have to wait to get served and chairs to sit on when the corns begin to play up. They'll have those super pneumatic change conveyors and everything will be reasonably priced in real money not this decimated nonsense.

There'll be smaller shops, too, with all the things we really want, like electrical gadgets that can be repaired when they go wrong. And somewhere to get them repaired, and a hearing-aid service centre – or two. Sugar, tea, dried fruit and so on, weighed out into bags. Butter, cheese and marge sold loose. Nails and screws sold by weight or number, in little twists of paper. Packets of fags split into singles and real beer in bottles.

Then it'll be time for a spot of lunch, which will probably be fish and chips out of newspaper, with perhaps ice-cream to follow, made by an Italian in a van and sold loose.

In the afternoon, a stroll down to the beach and a snooze in the sun. And later, a nice tray of tea on the beach, a toasted teacake and a real stick of barley sugar. In the distance there may be the genteel sound of a portable gramophone to which some polite young people are dancing the two-step. Or perhaps a real band playing on the bandstand.

In the evening there will be so many things to do. A dozen cinemas, all showing films that won't make anyone blush or have nightmares. Dance-halls with music that isn't too loud and has a tune. Pubs with real draught beer pulled by hand. Darts and dominoes, and crisps with blue bags of salt, and no muzak. If we're lucky, we may see a public hanging of a disc-jockey who talked over the music.

After such a full day of fun, back to the digs, where the good landlady will have prepared a mug of steaming Sanatogen at just the right temperature. And so to bed, with Radio 2 for company.

Luke Sherry, Lancs

· · ·

I am getting very excited about the TOGs Theme Park. I can see that this is going to be a great success.

The White-Knuckle Ride should be levelled off to give a nice smooth ride in comfortable coaches. When approaching the ride there should be a sign saying 'Due to leaves on the line and staff shortages, the White-Knuckle Ride may be subject to delays and cancellations'. This will make all TOGs feel immediately secure.

Then we ought to address ourselves to the Water Chute. Instead of being sprayed with icy cold water, as enjoyed by such young people as Princess Diana, we should be lowered gently into a steaming pool of quietly bubbling water and afterwards taken into a nearby hut where we can be rubbed down with some alcohol and a copy of *The Sporting Life*.

The Whip, instead of hurtling us around at sixty m.p.h in uncomfortable chairs, causing untold damage to our vertebrae, should be changed so that we can sit in huge patio-type swinging loungers with canopies reminiscent of Judy Garland in *Meet Me in St Louis*.

Instead of hamburger stalls we could have restaurants serving *haute cuisine*, such as *Fillet Steak Béarnaise* and *Noisettes du Lamb with Raspberry Sauce*, served with *Potatoes Dauphinoises*, all washed down with fine clarets and white Burgundy.

Yes. Yes. Yes. When does it open? Where can I buy a ticket? Where can I buy shares?

Alan Salsbury, Essex

*Not all were as madcap,
and careless of life and limb.*

Re the TOGs Theme Park. I don't really fancy hurtling down white-water rapids, even if it were followed by Sanatogen milkshakes!

Please could we have a Commode Carousel for the slightly less adventurous? The commodes could gently trundle around at five m.p.h., and could be decorated with jolly pictures of our own J.Y.

Avril Spencer, York

. . .

TOGS are game for anything but take it slowly. and preferably with a nice cuppa tea.

WHEN THE MAGIC Eye three-dimensional pattern pictures first emerged, they received short shrift from your straight-talking, no-nonsense TOG. 'I see no ships!' was the cry. 'Pretty patterns butter no parsnips!' was another. Piqued at their inability to spot the dolphins, unicorns and other flora and fauna hidden in these pictures, TOGs scoffed at the things as bogus, the products of over-wrought young minds. And rightly so. It was but the work of a moment for a talented listener to produce the definitive TOG Magic Eye Picture. It is reproduced here for your delight:

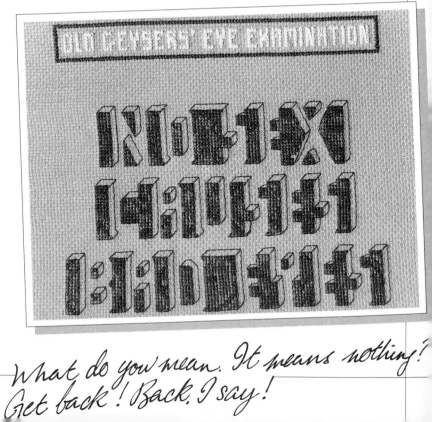

What do you mean. It means nothing! Get back! Back, I say!

· CHAPTER TWO ·

Dear Terry . . .

Dear Terry,

While lighting a Roman Candle at the weekend, it occurred to me that you could benefit your listeners immensely by following the firework code yourself, i.e.

1. LIGHT THE BLUE TOUCHPAPER.
2. RETIRE IMMEDIATELY.

(P.S. You can forget the bit about the blue touchpaper.)

Ivor Spital, Essex

TERRY WOGAN'S

I'M SUPPOSED TO have no feelings, of course . . . What is it with my crowd anyway? Every other Radio 2 presenter gets letters that are models of effusion and high-flown praise, extolling their professional and personal virtues. My post-bag is full to bursting with the barrage of contumely, the tirade of abuse, the assumed name, the false address . . .

. . .

Dear Terry,

Good morning. As Wimbledon approaches – how are you?

This conversation, re the above, took place recently between my offspring and myself.

Me (contemplating battered little radio): 'This has finally got to go.'

Son (fleetingly home for weekend): 'Oh, Mum, you can't bin that – all my childhood's in that radio. Switch it on and I'll be getting ready for school with Terry Wogan – and there'll be Björn Borg winning Wimbledon.'

Me: 'Where have you been? Didn't you know he's back.'

Son: 'Crikey!' (or words to that effect). 'Well, he won't get past the first round.'

Me: 'He might. He plays tennis with his doctor at the Albert Hall – he said so.'

Son: 'I thought he lived in Sweden!'

Yours sincerely,

Helen Highwater, N. Yorks

. . .

NOT ONLY ARE people confused –
they're not with us . . .

The Largest and Finest Steamers in the world

WHITE STAR LINE

"OLYMPIC" ✠ "TITANIC"

882½ FEET LONG   45,090 TONS REGISTER   92½ FEET BROAD

John P. Eaton and Charles A. Haas collection.

13 . 4 . 1912

DEAR TERRY.
YOUR RADIO SHOW
COMING THROUGH LOUD
AND CLEAR. GREAT TRIP.
GOOD BAND, AND
SUPERB FOOD.
THERE'S TALK OF ICE!
    REGARDS.
BRIAN NICHOLAS

THIS FATHER'S ... DAD A CARD

MR. T. WOGAN
BBC RADIO 2
    GILDEA ST.
BROADCASTING
HSE
LONDON W1.

RMS TITANIC, INC. COLLECTORS' SERIES

The Undead. And the lately departed.

Dear Mr Wogan,

*T*he undertaker found the attached note to yourself
under my late husband's body.
What does it mean? I never understood him.

Mrs Hopkinson

PHILIP HOPKINSON,
MIDDLESTOWN,
NR WAKEFIELD

Dear Terry,

I don't want to sound pompous, but I think that a lot
of the letters you have been reading lately have
lacked intellectual depth, and am sure you will
welcome a contribution from one of your more
thoughtful listeners.

Modesty almost forbids me from saying that I

Continued next page

have quite a reputation as a statistician and I'm sure
that all TOGs will be enthralled with the results of my
latest research project, which shows that most people
die aged between seventy and a hundred. Very few
people die aged over one hundred. I have checked and
rechecked my figures, and they are indisputable. So,
all we have to do is sort of tiptoe through these
dangerous years without attracting the attention of
the grim reaper. For myself, I contemplate thirty years
of safe sex and boneless fish.

Once through to the century, I intend to make up
for lost time as quickly as possible and would like to
invite all your female listeners currently aged under
three-and-a-half to the orgy. The mental picture

. . .

Bumper Book of TOGs

 THEY'RE DYING LIKE flies . . . Oft times, of an early morn, you'll find me propped up by Walter Wall's little 'zinc' bar at Hallam Street entrance of BBC Broadcasting House, preparing myself for the challenge of the programme ahead with a fortifying egg-nog and 'neath the manly tan and cheerful exterior, sick with worry. Are they all dead? Is there anybody out there? Can you hear me, Mother?

WOGAN'S OTHER LISTENER

I found him in the garden, he was lurking in the shed,
A little gnome-like fellow, with a flat cap on his head.
I said: 'What are you doing, where you've no right to be?'
He looked at me with mournful eyes, and said, 'Oh, pity me!
I'm Wogan's Other Listener . . . my name is Percy Pratt,
And I think the world of Terry – now what d'you say to that?'

He'd brought his little radio, some porridge and his tea,
And there among the cobwebs, like a fugitive sat he.
'They've driven me from home,' he sighed. 'I was afraid to stay,
In case they kept their promises, and had me put away.

You'd think I was a lunatic, or had some dread disease,'
Perce said, as Terry waffled on, as whacky as you please.

I felt so sad for Percy, that I told him he could stay,
He could bring his little radio, and hide there every day,
From half-past seven every morn, till Terry had to go
To do his proper daytime job – he has to eat, you know!
So Percy comes religiously, and even as I speak
He's hiding in my garden shed – he's there five days a week!

Poor Percy Pratt, now there's a man I never will forget,
But, as the Great One says himself, 'They're not all locked up yet!'

Kathleen Tuck, Cambs

I KNEW I sensed a presence . . . Then, just when you think it's safe to come out from behind the arras, your past rises up and deals you a thump to the mazzard.

. . .

Sir, you are a prump of the highest order and our dear beloved Queen would do well never to consider bestowing any kind of knighthood upon your wretched person.

We met, as you recall, that fateful summer during the annual carnival here in Hornsea. You were then a pathetic, penniless lingerie salesman fresh out of Ireland, travelling in ladies' underwear, destitute and homeless. Though against all odds still managing to keep warm in your thermal knickers.

I will never forget the day as we sat beneath a moonlit sky upon my fake walnut veranda as my feminine passions began to erupt within my heaving though somewhat stumpy bosom. 'Is there anything you would like to do for me?' I coyly asked.

'I've already chopped the firewood,' you announced. 'And gone to Tesco and done all the shopping.'

'No, you don't understand,' I continued, 'I am

Continued next page

TERRY WOGAN'S

ready now to be fulfilled as a woman.'
'Yes,' you said, 'I could do with a pint of Guinness myself.'
'Dearest,' I breathlessly uttered. 'Think of me as an overgrown herbaceous border eagerly awaiting a strong handsome gardener to come and wade through my undergrowth and de-flower my blooms.' It was at this point you got up, went over to the garden shed, took out a pair of shears and proceeded to dead-head every rose bush in sight . . .

Hilda Mugwump, Humberside

.   .   .

The old eyes playing you tricks again, eh, Hilda?
That wasn't me —
that was Alan O'Titchmarsh...

· CHAPTER THREE ·

Toggy Ails . . . and Nostalgs

I said, its him again on the wireless, dear

THE PAST IS another country. Unfortunately, for those of us brought up in this neck of the woods, it could be hell, particularly if you owned up to a weakness.

Dear Mr Wogan,

My grandmother used to say that a cold, catarrh or any chest complaint could be cleared up by having the offending chest rubbed with a brick.

David Hobson, Sheffield

. . .

 IT WOULD CERTAINLY take your mind off any minor complaints. This, too, seems an efficacious remedy.

I *recall my father blowing sulphur powder down our throats – for sore throats – and how well I remember my poor sister having a stiff neck – and my mother ironing it with a flat iron, over brown paper.*

Millicent Phillips, Middx

THAT BROWN PAPER saved a lot of lives. And to think they used to complain about the Spanish Inquisition! Some grannies could have taught Torquemada a thing or two.

Dear Terry,

Before the sagas of 'ills' go away, here's a couple of mine, not yet mentioned.

FOR WHOOPING COUGH Tar Rope –
a piece of rough ol' rope, soaked in tar – around your neck.

EARACHE An onion put in the hot ashes till
soft, and the kernel put in your ear, with a white cloth tied round your head.

I've had them all, and I'm still here seventy-five years on.

Irene Isaacs, Avon

. . .

THEY KNEW THEY WERE BORN

The thermogene vest has now vanished,
The oil and the camphor have gone,
A whole generation hardly dared cough,
In case a poultice (red hot) was slapped on.

All winter they smelt of old goose-grease,
Red-flannel they attempted to hide,
They were forced into a liberty bodice,
With a piece of brown paper inside.

In those days, Spring heralded freedom,
It was off with the hated attire,
The smelly brown paper was flung in the bin,
The poultice was chucked on the fire.

Then Summer arrived in its glory,
Hot days on the beach were a treat,
Resplendent in new knitted swimsuits,
They ran into the sea with bare feet.

But when water seeped into the swimsuit,
It caused it to droop and to sag,
The shoulders dropped down to the waistline,
It resembled an old carpet bag.

Tears and sobs and hysterics,
Accompanied the unfortunate child,
As it gathered the huge soggy garment,
And ran into the beach hut to hide.

Continued next page

No one ever considered their feelings,
They were children and knew where they stood,
They just put up and shut up and said naught,
All these things were done for their own good.

Avril Spencer, York

.   .   .

 COMPARED TO THE knitted swimsuit round your ankles, the tarred rope, the onion and the brick were only in the ha'penny place as instruments of torture . . .

But Heavens to Murgatroyd. Surely it wasn't *all* inhuman suffering and bread poultices! Did no light glimmer, however faintly, in the slough of despond?

Aga Saga

Dear Woggers,

*I*n my youth, a long time past,
my mater's AGA, blue and vast,
in kitchen stood, midst coke and wood,
trays of ash and pans of food,
sprinkled with dust, but smelling good.
I from school, in icy blast,
cycling home on roads like glass,
into kitchen dashing fast,
lean back on AGA, home at last;
There's nowt like AGA for warming arse.

Yours sincerely,

Nigel Wagstaffe (Waggers)

P.S. Many years ago you read out a letter of mine re a strange, grey, four-legged, bushy-tailed bird, which was taking food from a listener's bird-table. Did you ever discover what species it was?

. . .

 LORD LOVE YOU Waggers, it was the old ring-tailed sloth, a creature as familiar and well-loved to TOGs as the Thelwall Fireduck itself . . .

The running sore that was The Aga Saga was caused by the ageing thespian Jeremy Irons, who was observed by a keen-eyed TOG (is that an oxymoron?) in a hardware store in deepest Cotswoldshire inquiring after a small, bright part for his 'AAGAH'. Swift was the division into PRO and CON AAGAH factions. Slurs were cast on city-dwellers in Barbours and green wellies.

Word-pictures of bucolic bliss were freely painted, involving steak-and-kidney puddings, labradors, roasted squirrel and the like. People who should have known better waxed positively Betjemanesque:

I'm in love with my AGA-SAGA,
Oh yes I am,
With its warmth and affection
and thick-bottomed pan . . .
Oh, those cold, winter mornings
it throws out such heat –
as we sit by the oven
and put in our feet.
For drying our smalls –
it steams to perfection!
And every cake, bread and biscuit
is a wondrous confection.
I'm in love with my Aga –
you should get one dear Terry.
It's not just for the 'Hoorays'
and those with green welly –
you find things at the bottom
you've had there for weeks –
brown pieces of crust –
the odd sock, dried-out leeks.
Imagine the bonus
for you in the morning –
as downstairs you tumble
hung-over and yawning –
that warm friendly AGA
is waiting to greet you –
to crank-start your body
for the nation to meet you . . .

From the Well-trousered Viola Player,
as from the Royal Liverpool Philharmonic Orchestra

*Nah... Cup of the old builders tea, and I'm asright as Rain....
Sorry! Don't mention the Rain!*

A SPRING TIME POEM

*N*ow's the time that people spot
Crop-circles or a U.F.O.,
Or hope the Song for Europe
will be won by François Truffaut.
And Wogan fans ignore the rain
(for they're a plucky clan)
They know that sunshine only means
A NATIONAL HOSEPIPE BAN!

Jill Oxborrow, somewhere near Sunny Scunny

BUMPER BOOK OF TOGS

A SONG FOR spring. But as any Old Geezer or Gal knows, the sound of the first cuckoo is merely the harbinger of the January Sales, and an early warning of the vicissitudes of Yuletide.

Dear Terry,

So, the party season is upon us. Are you well seasoned yet? I'm still waiting to get pickled. So I am still able to send this verse:

If you can keep your feet when all about you
Are falling to the floor the worse for drink,
And wake up in the morning bright and cheerful
When all around are less than in the pink,
If you can recollect, in smallest detail,
What happened yesterday, and never blush,
And get your Christmas presents bought and parcelled
And never end up flustered in a rush,

If after every Yule and New Year party
You can face yourself, and friends with no regret,
Well, you must be some kind of festive smarty,
And frankly, I don't think I've met you yet!

Katie Mallett, Essex

. . .

 I FIND THE best plan is to keep yourself to yourself and avoid occasions of sin. And remember, it is no sin, if you don't take pleasure from it . . .

CHAPTER FOUR

Another Day Begins ...

'A thousand years, Chairman!'
'Floreat! Floreat.'
'A thousand years!'

THE SHOUTS AND cheers ring out from the serried ranks of bowler-hatted middle management, as the Great Coach of the BBC, drawn by its four proud, prancing, jet-black stallions, snorts and steams to a halt outside the mighty portals of Broadcasting House. A servile ostler scampers forward with the steps as the coach-door opens. A Byronic, patrician figure steps down. Even as he does, the bowler-hatted ranks prostrate themselves, kow-towing in the time-honoured fashion. The tall silver-haired figure with its great purple cloak, strides silently to the doors. A eunuch in the Director General's Court sidles up and whispers in the Great Man's ear: 'Remember, Dukie: you, too, are human . . .'

The Chairman has arrived. Another day at the BBC has begun . . .

. . .

Or so they would have you believe. The truth, as all TOGs know to their sorrow, is a much more mundane, nay tragic, tale.

The wind and rain lash relentlessly down the canyon of Regent Street, to crash thunderously against the creaking doors of Old Broadcasting House. Inside a roaring fire crackles merrily, reflected on the walls of rich mahogany, and glinting on the shimmering chandeliers of Waterford crystal. Along the wall a typical BBC Canteen breakfast buffet sits invitingly: larks' tongues, *Terrine de Foie*, *Kedgeree*, *Lamb Chops Reform*, *Baron of Beef*, *Kidneys Jerez*, eggs over-easy and sunnyside-up, chitterlings, Jabugo ham, Dublin Bay prawns, rashers . . . The receptionists and commissionaires help themselves from the groaning board.

''Ere, Maurice?'

'Yeah?'

'It's nine o'clock in the morning, shouldn't we open the doors?'

'Naah. It's taters out there, mate. Let 'em come in the tradesman's entrance . . .'

Outside, the wind and rain continue to hammer the gleaming pavements, thudding like tracer bullets into a collapsed cardboard box, in which a drenched decrepit figure sits, hunched against the elements. There is a sound of clinking bottles, as the ragged unfortunate moves to attract the attention of a passer-by. 'Spare us some dosh for a cuppa, Missus?'

Sarah Kennedy (for it is she), a vision in bombazine and Mechelen lace, with a mob-cap perched saucily on her golden curls, laughs merrily as she throws some change at the tragic figure:

'There you are, my man. Don't spend it on drink!'

The piteous bedraggled wreck scrabbles in the rain for the few pence.

'Gor bless yer ma'am. Gor bless yer . . .'

For Dukie, Chairman of the BBC, another day has begun . . .

· CHAPTER FIVE ·

A Song for ... the Corporation?

APART FROM THE tea-ladies and the commissionaires, the people who *really* run the BBC are a charming couple, Bert and Phyllis. Bert's full name is Bert Birt, and he's the Director General. Phyllis, his helpmeet and boon companion is, well, Phyllis.

This happy-go-lucky, unspoilt and down-to-earth couple were the popular hosts of a cheery and very popular pub, the Duck's Foot, in Fitzrovia, where they made quite a name for themselves with their fine English cheeses and crispy French bread.

The service and civility they experienced as regulars of the Duck's Foot so impressed the BBC's Board of Governors, that when the

running of the World's Greatest Broadcasting
Organization fell vacant, Bert and Phyllis
were the natural choices.

How well they have settled in! They
inspire great affection with their kindly ways,
and there is ever a homemade scone and a
bottomless tea-pot a-bubble for the passing
employee in their warm and welcoming
chintz-covered apartment on the fourth floor
of Broadcasting House.

Bert and Phyllis are up and about very
early, and can be seen most mornings, rain
or shine, as they jog the streets surrounding
the BBC in their matching shell suits.

A little song to accompany our two friends
on their morning jog, to be sung to the tune
of 'John Brown's Body'. . .

*O*ur names are Bert and Phyllis, and we've
not been here too long,
*To keep our workers happy, we are looking for a
song.*
*We need to show the listeners we're a happy
little throng,*
Busy working for the BBC.

I feel a total Birtin this shell suit, Phyllis!

Chorus:
We are wearing matching shellsuits,
We are wearing matching shellsuits,
We are wearing matching shellsuits,
And they glow as a we jog along.

Anon

. . .

THE SEARCH FOR a 'BBC Song' has been exhaustive, not to say exhausting. An anthem, a great inspirational hymn to send the BBC's employees marching down Regent Street, twenty-a-breast, arms-linked, like an old Gracie Fields movie. 'Sing As We Go, and Let the World Go By!'

The TOGs rose to meet this grand concept like rocketing pheasants.

From Hilda and Dilys Marvin of Cambridgeshire:

TO THE TUNE OF
'RULE BRITANNIA'

When Auntie fi-i-i-rst at REITH's Command
aro-o-o-ose from out of Portland Place,
arose, arose, arose from out of Portland Place,
this was their CHARTER to entertain the world,
and all the Staff are trained to sing this refrain:

Rule, dear Auntie
Dear Auntie rules air waves
The staff who work here always will be slaves.

 THE CORRECT TRIUMPHAL note – but inspirational? Might this offering, from Richard Holworthy from Dorset more readily fit the bill?.

. . .

I am much taken with the idea of a corporate song for the Corporation. It must have a British melody, be easy to sing and have a rousing and jolly refrain. May I offer the following, to be sung, con gusto, to the tune of 'Come Lassies and Lads':

Come lassies and lads, you mothers and dads,
Tune into the BBC
There's plenty for you on Radio 2
And culture on Radio 3.
With plays and a whole lot more
Of wonders on Radio 4
And for sport that's live we've Radio 5
We've something for all, you see.
And your licence pays for our winning ways
Hurrah for the BBC!

(Pause for a little gavotte)

Our children have fun with Radio 1
Tune into the BBC
Commercialise with our Enterprise
And snap up our tapes with glee
We give you a real choice
With chat show or mystery voice
A prize can be won with the big John Dunn
Or even with Simon Dee
And the Irish goon who can't sing in tune
Is part of our BBC.

. . .

Good ... but not the ending
I would have chosen ....

TERRY WOGAN'S

SOMETHING SIMPLER PERHAPS? What about this crowd-pleaser to the manly, upstanding strains of 'We are the Ovaltineys'?

Hey wake up — I've just thought of a corporate song for the Beeb — wanna hear it?

We are the BBC workers
Happy girls and boys,
We work all night,
We work all day,
We never have no time to play,
Then when our shift is finished
We go home to rest,
Then it's off to bed
To rest our head.
We work so hard,
We're almost dead.
So what more can be said,
We're working for the BBC.

THERE! THAT'S BETTER! Thank you, David J. Hunneybell of Northamptonshire.

Many a suggested anthem was inspired by *Snow White and the Seven Dwarfs*:

*H**i-ho, Hi-ho*
It's off to work we go.
We work for Birt,
For Birt we work,
Hi-ho, Hi-ho . . .
etc., etc.

You get the idea?

OTHERS WANTED SOMETHING more impressive, along the lines of 'Also Sprach Zarathustra' or Charpentier's 'Te Deum', but these suggestions didn't seem to sit well with the original Gracie Fields idea . . .

The anonymous and unaddressed Tryin' Ryan has a bright thought:

.   .   .

What I suggest is that, like happy Japanese workers at the beginning of their shift, you sing in praise of the leaders of the Corporation. And do you know, when you recite the names of your leaders, there's a cadence that at once suggests a particular tune?

Just recite this, and the tune is apparent:

Yentob, Yentob, Yentob, Yentob, Yentob, Forgan and Birt.
Yentob, Yentob, Yentob, Forgan and Birt – Forgan and Birt.
Yentob, Yentob, Yentob, Yentob, Yentob, Forgan and Birt.
Yentob, Yentob, Yentob, Forgan and Birt – Forgan and Birt.

Du-ukie, Dukie, Dukie, Dukie, Chairman for a thousand years,
Chairman for a thousand years, Dukie-eee, Dukie, Dukie, Dukie.
Du-uke, Dukie, Dukie, Dukie, Chairman for a thousand years.
Chairman for a thousand years, thousand years.

. . .

A RABBLE-ROUSER TO lift morale in the blood-bolstered corridors and studios of BH and TVC, and strike fear and loathing among the denizens of ITV, IRN, ITN, LWT, YTV and, for all I know, B&Q, GKN and ICI.

Terry's leaving!

FULL STORY FROM YOUR ROVING REPORTER

I n shock news released last week it was discovered that Terry Wogan is leaving the BBC to pursue his career elsewhere. Sources within the BBC refused to state whether Terry was leaving of his own free will or whether there is a scandal surrounding the drastic news. Our reporters have been ringing the BBC non-stop for the last ten days, but as usual nobody could be bothered to answer the phone.

This latest departure comes in the wake of other well known and

loved staff who have left recently. Sid, admired for his tireless work in the BBC toilets, left under a cloud recently. Three days earlier Frank Godfrey's masseur was seen leaving in tears after he was found in a compromising position with Jimmy Young's favourite young nurse.

Your reporter went to Bert's

Bistro late today to try and get the inside story. He met secretly with a well known newsreader and womaniser who asked to remain nameless, but

Join our Fantasy Newsreaders league.
(See page 7)

we will call 'The Voice of the Balls'. Trying to get to the bottom of the story proved difficult because 'Balls' was obviously under the influence of excessive amounts of alcohol and was busy writing love letters to someone with the initials F.G. Later that same evening the gorgeous Frank Godfrey arrived with her huge entourage of hangers on. She was dressed, as usual, in a tight but flimsy bodice and fashionable thigh length boots. When asked about the rumours of Terry's demise she was heard to say 'Who? Do I know him, hith name theem to wing a bell but I can't thay I can we-call hith faith. Now sthop peering down the top of my flimthy blouthe or I'll call the polithe!' Long queues of angry listeners have been seen in the BBC reception area in recent days, so nothing new there!

We will keep you informed of any new developments as they arise, meanwhile see the special commemorative feature of Terry later in this issue.

Summer is coming!

With the summer season approaching, the BBC Board of Directors has finalised the new staff summer uniforms. A special staff preview will take place on Thursday 6th April in the BBC canteen. It is an effort to not only keep cool this summer, but to attract more listeners to visit the BBC. It will also be more functional for specific jobs. To this end all of the new uniforms will be job-related. Receptionists and Bert's Bistro staff will dressed in skimpy new silk uniforms, skirts will be twelve inches above the knee and the whisper-thin blouses will plunge daringly down to the navel. Underclothing will be from the new

Frank Godfrey sheer silk collection and will complement the newly designed uniforms, particularly because it is so brief. The glasses behind the bar area will all be stored at knee level to encourage staff to bend down more. Male members of staff will be issued with Lurex boxer shorts and a black bow tie.

BBC Canteen staff will have similar uniforms for serving evening meals, although they will be made of a washable fabric. All female members of staff affected will be invited to attend special classes to learn how to walk seductively in the new six inch high stiletto heels.

BBC kitchen uniform

BBC kitchen staff will be issued with new and more effective gas masks and chemical-resistant gloves to make it safer to handle the food. All staff meals will now be bought in from an outside source to cut down on staff absence due to illness. BBC Governors will continue to bring sandwiches. A larger plate is being designed and kept especially for when Terry Wogan visits the canteen to stop his constant moaning about the amount of chips he gets and to prevent him having his food served directly on a tray. Staff are continually amazed at the amount of food he eats even

This week TOG Lottery numbers.

T he newly launched TOG lottery was launched this week. First prize in the lottery is a brand new 1966 Volvo Estate in Sunburst yellow. The winning numbers are as follows.

6	32	6.5	22	22	0

All claims should be made within seven days to avoid confusion.

though he remains slim, lithe and never puts on an ounce. Cleaning staff will also be issued with new uniforms. They will wear Chemical Warfare suits for cleaning out studios used by Radio 1 staff.

Pamela Anderson to be replaced on Baywatch!

Frank Godfrey

R umour is rife that Frank Godfrey has been offered the job as replacement for Pamela Anderson in the next series of Baywatch. Frank was unavailable for comment last night because she was running around the countryside opening fete's supermarkets and various other meetings.

Popularity Poll

A poll at last week's BBC Producers Dinner/Dance & Pub crawl – BBC staff were used to test the popularity of Producer 'Paulie' Paul Walters, that back room aficionado of all things 'Toggie'. It seems that 50 per cent of those present did not like him, while the other 50 per cent had never met him.

Wildlife at the BBC?

In last month's newsletter we had an article about Pandas. It explained how they are very fussy about what they eat, they are bad tempered, you hardly ever see them and they hardly ever make love. A letter was sent to the editor saying that apparently three Pandas work in BBC reception.

Thoughts for the day...

Beauty is in the eye of the beerholder...

There are 3 kinds of people: those who can count and those who can't.

Why is "abbreviation" such a long word?

Don't use a big word where a diminutive one will suffice.

I can see clearly now the brain is gone ...

The beatings will continue until morale improves.

I used up all my sick days, so I'm calling in dead.

If one synchronized swimmer drowns, do the rest have to drown too?

Shin: A device for finding furniture in the dark.

Dain bramaged.

Phil Boulter
pab@kcc.co.uk.

Classified Section

SECTION 1
Lost and Found

Found, large orange duster and other cleaning materials, hardly used, possibly belonging to BBC cleaning staff.

Found, book called 'How to become a successful BBC lottery announcer' with written dedication on first page 'To Alan, good luck from Mummy'.

SECTION 2
Sits Vac

Telepath wanted: you know where to reply.

DJ required for early morning show on Radio 2. No previous experience required. Apply to M Hussey with full C.V.

Female Newsreader required to replace one from the BBC who is getting too busy with personal appearances to actually do her job.

SECTION 3
Services

Ears pierced while you wait, ring 0123 456 7890

Fetes supermarkets and other things opened by well known BBC celebrity. Apply to Frank Godfrey @BBC.org.uk

$\left(\cdot \ \text{CHAPTER SIX} \ \cdot \right)$

Bodice-ripping Sagas

 'BUT,' I HEAR you cry, 'surely the BBC is *more* than Berts and Phyllises, Forgans and Yentobs.' Courage Camille! Of course it is. There are Marsh, Dedicoat and Godfrey, too. Or as we TOGs know them, Jean Marsh, Deadly Alancoat and Frank Godfrey. Three pivotal figures in the swirling whirligig that constitutes life at the BBC.

JEAN MARSH is not to be confused with the distinguished actress of the same name, though he would like to be. Nor, indeed, the French actor Jean Marais, Jean Cocteau's friend. Marsh never even met Cocteau! Marsh is a demented organist, along the lines of Dr Phibes, who has cleared more halls than any dozen alternative comedians.

DEADLY ALANCOAT, also known as the Voice of the Balls, is a graceless youth of surly demeanour from Redditch or Dudley. A Balti purist, he believes this sub-continental dish can only be properly savoured when licked off a dirty floor somewhere in the cantonments of Birmingham. Rarely seen without two paper bags over his head.

FRANK GODFREY – descendant of Private Godfrey, the incontinent old soldier of *Dad's Army* fame. Her merry tinkling laugh frightens livestock and causes strong men to shiver. Godfrey's veneer of gormless innocence masks a steely heart; men are her playthings, to be used, then cast aside like a worn-out glove. Last year she threw her own mother out.

For reasons into which it may not be even healthy to enquire, these three unfortunates are cast as the main players in a series of

Victorian melodramas or 'Bodice-rippers', in which the lead role is played by the cruel and perverted Baron de Wogan, based on some appalling despot whose name escapes me. The minor roles are filled, as usual, by Dukie, Birt and Phyllis, who don't seem able to let *anything* go in the BBC without interfering.

. . .

★ ★

PLOT FOR

BODICE-RIPPER

STARRING
FRAN GODFREY
AND OTHERS

PART III

★ ★

In the baronial hall of Schloss Woganberg stands the tall, arrow-straight figure of Baron de Wogan. The flickering candlelight shows the cruel smile playing across his finely chiselled features and Birt and Phyllis, his guards, cringe as he slaps his riding crop against his top-boots.

Birt and Phyllis hold between them a struggling Fran Godfrey, whom they have dragged from the dungeon at the Baron's order.

de Wogan: *'Take young Frank to der shower room. Zwer are matters I wish to discuss mit him.'*

Fran: *'Never, you brute! For I have given my heart to another, my beloved Jean Marsh!'*

Suddenly with a fanfare the doors burst open and a

figure in an old mackintosh tied with string shuffles in. De Wogan falls on one knee crying: 'A thousand years, Dukie!'

Dukie: *''Ere, Tel, noice gaff yer got 'ere. Better than me cardboard box. Nah, oi come to take that Fran Godfrey away wiv me, and being as how oi'm a duke an' you're only a baron oi'm gonna pull rank on you. Come along darlin' . . . oi'll get a tea-chest for you to live in.'*

de Wogan (hissing): *'Curses! Foiled again!'*

Anon

. . .

Don't leave us with a cliff hanger! This is not some Australian soap-opera!

★ ─────────────────────────────── ★

THE
FRAN GODFREY

BLOCKBUSTING
BODICE-RIPPER

PART IV

★ ─────────────────────────────── ★

THE STORY SO FAR . . .

Fran, a gorgeous, pouting ex-lingerie model has fallen in love with Jean Marsh, a grotesquely deformed organ player kept locked up in the dungeons of Schloss Woganberg, family seat of the handsome, dashing cad and out-and-out bounder, Baron de Wogan. De Wogan has been foiled in his attempt to discuss manly matters in the shower with Fran by the sudden arrival of Dukie, who has whisked Fran off to his cardboard box outside Broadcasting House. Now read on . . .

Dukie: "'Ere, Fran, 'ave a swig of this cider, s'absolutely brilliant, much better than that meths yesterday.'

Fran: 'Oh, Dukie Sir, you're so kind to have rescued me from that cruel, heartless Baron de Wogan. However I'm not sure if I'm really a cardboard-box person . . . There's hardly any space for me to hang my underwear and besides I do miss my beloved Jean. After that beastly Deadly Alancoat left me I thought I was going to die, until I met Jean. A pity about his appearance, though.'

Suddenly they hear a sharp knock on the cardboard. Enter Jean Marsh.

Fran: 'Jean! My darling, but how you've changed! You look so . . . manly!'

Jean: 'I know! Thanks to Gloria Hunniford's magic spell I now have a body of a twenty-year-old athlete. She even offered to repair my organ! However, my dearest, it has made me see that there is more to life than love . . . There are organs to be played, bannisters to be built . . . And besides, I'm married already. Adieu, my love!'

Fran: 'But did you not love me?'

Jean: 'Dearly, my Fran. But now I don't give a damn.'

THE END

Anon

And you think that's as bad as it gets?

★ ★

THE BODICE-RIPPER SAGA

Starring Fran Godfrey
and featuring
a Cast of Thousands

★ ★

ACT XXII, SCENE 15

When Baron de Wogan awakes he discovers he is chained to the slime-covered walls of the dungeon, completely naked except for his monocle and cigarette holder, at the end of which sputters a Woodbine.

He looks down the dungeon: there are chained bodies as far as he can see. The chains next to him rattle and a familiar voice says, 'Allo, Tel, me old cocker! Wot you doin' 'ere then? Cor, oim dying for a cider . . .'

'Silence!' a cruel shrill voice rings out. 'Prisoners are not permitted to speak!'

Baron de Wogan shudders. There before him stands Fran Godfrey with a six-foot bullwhip in her hand. She wears thigh boots and her heaving bosom strains against the flimsy fabric of her bodice. Suddenly a button flies off and whistles past the Baron's ear.

Fran cracks the whip and murmurs in a silky voice: 'Now let the torture begin!'

TO BE CONTINUED

Anon

. . .

Can nobody bring this travesty to a climax?

RIPPING BODICES

THE CONCLUDING EPISODE OF THE WIDELY-ACCLAIMED BLOCKBUSTER SERIAL

Starring Fran Godfrey

WITH CAMEO PERFORMANCE BY

Terence O'Wogan

Fran eyes Jean Marsh with a haughty stare and brings her whip down across his grotesquely twisted body. Blow after blow rains upon his quivering flesh.

'I say,' says Jean, 'that's rather nice. Could you do it a bit more to the left, though?'

Baron de Wogan can stand it no longer, and with one bound he is free.

'Stop it, you flame-haired hussy!' he barks, 'Or I

will give you the cruellest torture in the castle,
listening to a non-stop recording of Jimmy Young
singing "The Man From Laramie"!'

'You will never take me alive!' cries Fran, and
dashes up the circular staircase to the top of the tower.

Swiftly the gallant Baron frees the captives and
they all run after the evil torturess. When they reach
the top they find Fran standing on the parapet.

'Goodbye, cruel world!' she cries. Several more
buttons fly off her bodice, making everyone duck. She
plunges towards the murky depths of the castle moat
and its waiting crocodiles and there is total silence.
And then . . . a ghostly giggle floats up through the
air . . .

THE END

Anon

.   .   .

 THERE WERE THOUSANDS of bodice-
ripping yarns, the vast majority of them
unprintable before the watershed.

That's the trouble with my crowd: they get
carried away. Usually by quiet, strong men in
white coats . . .

· CHAPTER SEVEN ·

What's the Fillum?

OFT TIMES, IN a pathetic attempt to hold the attention of the few remaining listeners still alive, not to mind awake, we have A Competition! There are no prizes, because this is *your* BBC and *you're* not made of money. Let the vulgar, crass commercial side of broadcasting offer £10 000 to anyone prepared listen to their dross, it's just not our style. It's the taking part that counts, after all. We've always favoured the Corinthian style. Training for the Olympics with a glass of Champagne balanced on each hurdle – trotting out to play the Arsenal at Wembley in tennis shirts and baggy shorts, having carelessly flicked away a Du Maurier cigarette in the tunnel . . . That sort of thing . . . Open the microphone, damn the torpedoes . . . I'll have a mug of cocoa in my sea cabin, Snotty, wake me if you see Jerry . . .

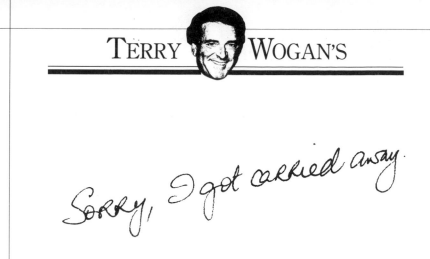
Sorry, I got carried away.

Anyway, this Competition. It wasn't really A Competition, just something that developed out of a spontaneous combustion of its own. It just *happened*, okay? Who can explain it, who can tell you why, fools give you reasons, wise men etc., etc. They called it *What's The Fillum?* and the answers are upside-down, the way God intended . . .

· · ·

Mellors (in potting shed). 'It's no good, my lady, it's wilting.'

Lady Chatterley: 'Oh, dear, what's caused that?'

Mellors: 'I think the frost got it, my lady.'

Lady Chatterley: 'Oh, Mellors, what can we do?'

Mellors: 'I'm sorry, my lady, I think we'll have to abandon the banana trees and plant something more hardy.'

WHAT'S THE FILLUM?

ANSWER: BACK TO THE FUSCHIA

Katie Mallett, Essex

There's no Fuschia for us Mellors, if that's all you can produce

TERRY  WOGAN'S

SCENE: remote trading post, Kenya, 1901
A tall young woman enters. She is wearing
riding clothes and a pith helmet. She speaks
with a hint of a Danish accent.

Woman: 'Good morning. I would like some paprika,
please.'

Proprietor: 'I am sorry, we don't have any.'

Woman: 'Oh, no, I'm making a goulash. I've ridden
twenty miles . . . You must have *some* paprika . . .'

Proprietor: 'None at all, madam. Sorry.'

WHAT'S THE FILLUM?

ANSWER: OUT OF PAPRIKA

Phil O'Sann, London

· · ·

Let me spell it out lady – P..A..F..P..R..I..K.A – Paprika

But there's no 'F' in Paprika

That's what I'm trying to tell you

Footsteps. Door opens.
(German accent) 'Are you in zer? Nein? Okay.'
Door closes. Footsteps. Door opens.
(German accent) 'Are you in here zen? Nein? Okay.'
Door closes. Footsteps. Heels click.
(German accent) 'I am sorry, mein Kapitan, I cannot
find him anyvair.'

WHAT'S THE FILLUM?

ANSWER: SCHINDLER'S LOST.

Jan Cowan, Kent

. . .

'Did you have a nice holiday?' asked Fred.

'Not really,' said Wilf. 'We went to a little seaside place
in Ireland, just along the coast from Belfast. All the
time I had the feeling that I was being followed, but
each time I glanced back, there was no-one there.'

WHAT'S THE FILLUM?

ANSWER: LOOK BACK IN BANGOR

Tony Barham, Avon

. . .

'Terrific steak-and-kidney pie,' cried the man. 'But where's me pommes frites?'

WHAT'S THE FILLUM?

ANSWER: GOOD PIE MISSED THE CHIPS

David Little, Essex

. . .

Dukie pops into the studio and says: "'Allo Tel-boy, me old mucker. 'Ow yer doin', me old son? 'Ere – I watched a video last night called *Barbarella*. Cor – the bird that played the main part is one sexy piece, ain't she? I'd really fancy a slap-and-tickle session wiv that one – know what I mean, Tel. Eh? Eh?"

WHAT'S THE FILLUM?

ANSWER: A WISH CALLED FONDA

Ken-Ivor Wutwac, Essex

. . .

BUMPER BOOK OF TOGS

Old Geezer: 'It's getting more and more difficult to get up in the mornings – what with the rheumatics 'n' all.'

Old Gal: 'In that case, I'll wait till you've had lunch to take you to the theme park.'

WHAT'S THE FILLUM?

ANSWER: TOG DAY AFTERNOON

Jill Oxborrow, Sunny Scunny

.   .   .

'Thank you,' said the new President, 'that was a very good abdication speech, your Ex-Majesty. 'By the way, when you empty the palace, please make sure you take all those shiny suits with you.'

WHAT'S THE FILLUM?

ANSWER: LAST OF THE MOHAIR KINGS

David Perrott, Cambridgeshire

.   .   .

TERRY WOGAN'S

S cene: Carlton Home for the crinkled and creased, where the high point of the day is watching Batty Hilda trying to break through the skin on her mug of Ovaltine.

The Matron is addressing the monthly meeting of the 'Action for TOGs' Group where questions are debated, such as: why, if the bulk of the population qualify as listeners to the Terry Wogan show, is the print in newspapers so small?

Anyway, Matron asks the assembled grey power where they should go for this month's day out in the charabanc. Batty Hilda's friend, Ida Lovitt, suggests they go to the Lady Bower Dam as that's where she did her courting.

WHAT'S THE FILLUM?

ANSWER: RESERVOIR TOGS

Ron Gretton, Notts

.   .   .

And one more from
the T.O.G. cartoonist..

Moo

Moo to you too

'BEEF ENCOUNTER'

Nobody said it was going
to be easy . . . . . .

$\cdot$ CHAPTER EIGHT $\cdot$

TOGs Like Rhymes, Okay?

IT'S NO USE looking at *me*! TOGs are people who want to know how time flies like an arrow, but fruit flies like a banana . . . TOGs shudder at the very name of Kirsty Ambridge, the terrifying West Indian fast bowler, and are transfixed with fear by that huge All Black who tramples other rugby players into the ground, Joanna Lumley . . .

Here is a typical TOG joke, from Pauline Lynch of Norfolk:

$\cdot$ $\cdot$ $\cdot$

'*My dog's got no nose!*'
'*Pardon?*'
'*My dog's got no nose!*'
'*Oh! How does he smell?*'
'*What?*'
'*How does he smell?*'
'*A quarter-past three.*'

· · ·

LATER, THE SAME JOKE...

I've now got the most expensive hearing-aid money can buy.

What kind is it?

About five thirty

DOG WITH NO NOSE →

You had to be there...

Don't ask me who started the updated nursery rhyme thing, but it made for many hours of innocent enjoyment:

Hickory dickory dock,
The mouse ran up the clock.
The clock struck one
But Rentokil would not come out
in the middle of the night.

Hey diddle diddle,
The cat and the fiddle,
The cow jumped over the moon –
The poor thing had mad cow's disease.

Jack and Jill went up the hill
To fetch a pail of water
Jack fell down
And broke his crown
And had to wait three months for an NHS bed.

Anon

. . .

Little Miss Muffet
Sat on a tuffet
Eating her box of Milk Tray
Down came an old geezer
Who started to squeeze her
And now he's been done
for sexual harassment.

*If all the world were paper.
And all the sea were ink,
Rupert Murdoch would control the lot.*

*Little fishes in a brook.
Father caught them on a hook.
Mother fried them in a pan,
National Rivers Authority prosecuted him for
fishing without a licence.*

Neil Bonnaud, Dyfed

Little Jack Horner sat in a corner
Eating a Eurofruit pie.
He put in his thumb and pulled out a plum –
He knew it was a plum because the sticker said so.

Geoff Snell

.   .   .

Old King Cole was a merry old soul,
and a merry old soul was he,
but he soon stopped laughing when the
Shadow Heritage Secretary moved him in
to a three-bedroomed semi.

Tom, Tom the piper's son,
Stole a pig and away he run.
He was subsequently arrested and
sent to Center Parcs for a holiday.

Peter Nesbitt, Humberside

.   .   .

$\cdot$ CHAPTER NINE $\cdot$

Now You See It ... Now You Don't

THE TOGS NOTICEBOARD is the brilliant invention of one Mary from Tideswell, or as she phonetically prefers it 'Tidza'. Like all the best ideas, it is stunning in its simplicity:

A simple Blackboard placed just behind my head, on which Old Poorly, the ailing but still game producer and infuser of builders' tea, writes in his ill-formed hand various messages at the behest of TOGs and other unfortunates.

The Noticeboard is a boon to the busy broadcaster: no more the repetitious braying of E-mail, fax and postal addresses. They're up there on the Noticeboard for all to see, renewed very day in different-coloured chalks, in order to prevent Zeitgeist, or boredom. Many other messages are placed there, mostly by young men with their baseball caps on back to front, advertising various foreign language lessons, and sessions with stern disciplinarians.

Brian Hornsby of Balsall Common was among the first to crave space on the Board, with typical TOG kindliness on behalf of a chum:

. . .

Would you please be good enough to put the following on your Noticeboard. It's not for me you understand but for a friend. His name is Peter Smith but he wants to remain anonymous!

```
═══ WANTED ═══

GOOD WOMAN

MUST BE ABLE TO CLEAN,
COOK, SEW, DIG WORMS
AND CLEAN FISH

MUST HAVE BOAT AND
MOTOR

PLEASE SEND PICTURE OF
BOAT AND MOTOR
```

Dear Tel,

I hope you like this scratch 'n' sniff fax. I thought if you put it on the Noticeboard, then everybody could get a whiff of the country. Also I'm faxing this in pink to match the chalk.

. . .

WHO ELSE, BUT the indefatigable Franki Thingy of Somewhere Up There Past Hadrian's Wall?

Then David Goodwin of York, a TYG with ambitions beyond his station, had a brainwave. He was about to marry the unfortunate Rose – Why not use the Board for their wedding list?

. . .

David and Rose's WEDDING LIST

1. His and Hers matching zimmer frames.

2. Grand Master TOG board game.

3. Gift vouchers for the TOGs Theme Park.

4. Gift vouchers for 'Easifit Dentures'.

5. The Spinners' Complete Collection.

6. Video: 'Mary Poppins 2 – The Revenge'.

7. A year's subscription to SAGA magazine.

8. The Greatest Hit of Terry Wogan – double CD!

9. Six issues of the TOG newspaper *The Togograph*.

10. His and Hers matching Jaguar XJS (dark-green).

. . .

I told the old fool that taking a year's subscription to SAGA magazine would be tempting fate.

 NO GREAT IDEA is without its drawbacks, of course, and the Noticeboard did present some local difficulties.

. . .

*M*ay I request that for those TOGs who are now a little less able to hear (going deaf as my wife so kindly puts it) could you please write any information on your Blackboard in LARGE BLOCK CAPITALS. This will help no end.

Ken Ross, Bucks

. . .

When I peer into the loudspeaker of my wireless with my right eye I can read every word clearly on your Blackboard (especially when you use your tartan chalk) but when I use my left eye there's nothing? Could it be that my radio is not stereo?

Mike Scott, Tyne & Wear

. . .

I'm getting fed up with all this talk of the Blackboard behind you and the interesting messages written on it. People in different parts of the country want you to move to one side or the other so they can see it and you're bobbing around like a wild thing.

Well, I don't think it's fair. I've never been able to see the Board – I'm only four-feet-ten-and-a-bit, and whatever part of the country I'm in I can't see over or around you.

But I don't want you to think I'm just a whinger so I have a potential solution which can help everyone, everywhere in the known world.

Put an extension cable on your '**cans**' (that's the right jargon, isn't it?) and then during every other record wheel your chair right out of the way and go and have a little chat with Pauly.

(Doing this would even give the Australians time to read it!)

Pam, Mid-Glamorgan

. . .

I'M DUCKING, BOBBING and weaving like Barry McGuigan in a corner, and they're *still* not satisfied! More timely tips.

. . .

Your listeners appear to be experiencing considerable difficulty in seeing the Noticeboard. I have a great idea to solve the problem. With a little reorganization of the studio the Board could be positioned in front of you and would thus become clearly visible to all. The fact that you would not longer be seen would not be a problem (some might even consider this an advantage) as you now appear regularly on television again.

TOGs with bad eyesight would find this particularly beneficial.

Eric Winning, Glos

. . .

What makes me suspect a hidden agenda?

Nothing behind-hand about *this* back-stabber – how would *you* like to get this little knife-in-the-small-ribs, with a covering note from my beloved Chairman?

Tel – me old mucker.
This looks like it's come from one of those eejits wot listens to you – y'know one of those DOGs or whatever you call 'em. (You are still doin' your programme, ain't yer?)
Do us a favour and deal with it, will yer?

Ta.

Dukie

. . .

Dear D-G,

I am a little concerned that at least one of your senior, distinguished radio presenters is on forbidden substances. No names, no pack drill, but there's a chap in the morning who's hallucinating.

It started when he thought he had more than one listener. Now he keeps making up imaginary secret signs. *And* he thinks he's got a noticeboard behind him. Perhaps you should send him on leave for a while? It must be three or four weeks since he had a break.

. . .

AH, JOHN HOWELL of Bromley Common! Or Lucrezia Borgia, as you will be known from now on . . .

As always with the TOGs, there are those (probably the majority) who miss the point, like Peregrine Falcon of Huddersfield.

I thought I'd write to say how excited I was to hear you had a blackbird in your studio.

Not only that, but now you have an Orange Hawk and the very rare Purple Hawk.

If I were a blackboard I wouldn't whistle, I'd screech.

That was blackboard, Perry. And chalk...

I give up... Nurse!...

The screens!... Too late...